GAO

Report to Congressional Committees

I0426389

September 2005

U.S.-CHINA TRADE

The United States Has Not Restricted Imports under the China Safeguard

GAO

Accountability * Integrity * Reliability

GAO-05-1056

Highlights

Highlights of GAO-05-1056, a report to congressional committees

September 2005

U.S.-CHINA TRADE

The United States Has Not Restricted Imports under the China Safeguard

Why GAO Did This Study

In joining the World Trade Organization (WTO) in December 2001, China agreed to a number of mechanisms to allow other WTO members to address disruptive import surges from that country. Among these was a transitional product-specific safeguard. In general, safeguards are temporary import restrictions of limited duration that provide an opportunity for domestic industries to adjust to increasing imports. U.S. law includes a number of other safeguards including a communist country safeguard, known as "section 406," and a global safeguard, known as "section 201," which have both applied to China.

In light of increased concern about Chinese trade practices and the U.S. government response to them, the conference report on fiscal year 2004 appropriations requested that GAO review the efforts of U.S. government agencies responsible for ensuring free and fair trade with that country. In this report, which is one of a series, GAO (1) describes the China safeguard, (2) describes how it has been used thus far, and (3) examines issues related to the President's discretion to apply the safeguard. Other safeguards provide context to understand this mechanism.

We provided ITC and USTR a draft of this report for their review and comment. Both agencies chose to provide technical comments from their staff. We incorporated their suggestions as appropriate.

www.gao.gov/cgi-bin/getrpt?GAO-05-1056.

To view the full product, including the scope and methodology, click on the link above. For more information, contact Loren Yager at (202) 512-4347 or yagerl@gao.gov.

What GAO Found

The China safeguard permits WTO members, including the United States, to address disruptive import surges from China. In the United States, the China safeguard is implemented under section 421 of the Trade Act of 1974, which allows U.S. firms to petition for relief and establishes a three-step process. This process involves the International Trade Commission (ITC), Office of the U.S. Trade Representative (USTR), and the President and determines whether Chinese imports are causing market disruption to domestic producers and whether a remedy is in the national economic interest. The entire process takes about 150 days. Under the terms of China's WTO accession agreement, WTO members may use the China safeguard until 2013.

To date, the United States has not applied the China safeguard in five cases brought by domestic producers. In a sixth case, ITC has not yet reached a decision. In two cases, ITC found no market disruption. In three cases, ITC found market disruption and USTR evaluated the pros and cons of various options and made a recommendation to the President. In all three cases, the President declined to provide relief to the domestic industry after he found it would not be in the national economic interest because the costs would outweigh the benefits. The success rate for China safeguard petitions is similar to communist country safeguard petitions, but differs from that of global safeguard petitions.

The President's decisions not to provide import relief after ITC found market disruption generated controversy, including a lawsuit claiming that he exceeded his authority. The relevant House committee intended that the law create a presumption in favor of relief upon an ITC injury finding. Nonetheless, the U.S. Court of International Trade found the President has broad discretion not to apply a China safeguard. Moreover, the President considers the question of whether to provide relief from a broader perspective than ITC. The President weighs the benefits of relief against the costs and considers factors such as the effect on consumers and downstream users, which ITC does not. The President cited third-country imports in all his decisions denying relief under both the Chinese and communist country safeguards. Under the global safeguard, third-country imports generally cannot diminish the potential benefits of import relief to the domestic industry and the President has often provided relief, especially since 1988 when U.S. trade laws were revised.

Outcomes of Completed China Safeguard Petitions (as of September 2005)

Product name	ITC vote on market disruption	Presidential determination
Pedestal actuators	3-2 in favor	Rejected 3-year quota
Wire hangers	5-0 in favor	Rejected 3-year additional duty
Brake drums and rotors	4-0 against	N/A
Waterworks fittings	6-0 in favor	Rejected 3-year tariff rate quota
Mattress innersprings	6-0 against	N/A

Sources: GAO, ITC, and presidential documents.

_____ **United States Government Accountability Office**

Contents

Abbreviations

ITC	International Trade Commission
TPSC	Trade Policy Staff Committee
USTR	Office of the United States Trade Representative
WTO	World Trade Organization

GAO

Accountability * Integrity * Reliability

United States Government Accountability Office
Washington, DC 20548

September 29, 2005

The Honorable Richard C. Shelby
Chairman
The Honorable Barbara A. Mikulski
Ranking Member
Subcommittee on Commerce, Justice, and Science
Committee on Appropriations
United States Senate

The Honorable Frank R. Wolf
Chairman
The Honorable Alan B. Mollohan
Ranking Member
Subcommittee on Science, State, Justice and
   Commerce, and Related Agencies
Committee on Appropriations
House of Representatives

Imports from China have grown rapidly over the last decade, from a total
value of about $42 billion in 1995 to over $196 billion in 2004.[1] While
lowering U.S. prices, and therefore benefiting consumers, this growth has
presented a major challenge for U.S. producers that compete with Chinese
products in the U.S. market.

In joining the World Trade Organization (WTO) in December 2001, China
agreed to a number of unique import relief mechanisms. Among them was
a transitional product-specific safeguard (China safeguard) that allows
other members to impose import restraints (such as quotas or tariffs) on
China in the event of disruptive import surges.[2]

In light of increased concern about Chinese trade practices and the U.S.
government response to them, the conference report on fiscal year 2004
appropriations legislation[3] requested that GAO monitor the efforts of U.S.

---

[1]Both values are expressed in constant 2004 dollars.

[2]WTO Protocol on the Accession of the People's Republic of China, art. 16.

[3]H.R. Rep. No. 108-401, at 574 (2003).

GAO-05-1056 U.S.-China Trade

government agencies responsible for ensuring free and fair trade with that country. In subsequent discussions with staff from the House Appropriations Committee's Subcommittee on Science, State, Justice and Commerce, and Related Agencies, we agreed to provide a number of reports on relief mechanisms available to U.S. producers who are adversely affected by unfair or surging imports and the manner in which these mechanisms have been applied to China.[4] In this report we (1) describe the China safeguard, (2) describe how the safeguard has been used thus far, and (3) examine issues related to the President's discretion to apply the safeguard.

To describe the safeguard, we reviewed U.S. laws and procedures as well as relevant WTO agreements. We interviewed staff members from the Office of the U.S. Trade Representative (USTR), the U.S. International Trade Commission (ITC), WTO officials, and other experts on trade law. In describing how the safeguard has been used thus far, we reviewed the official case records for each of the five completed safeguard investigations conducted by ITC and USTR. To clarify the views of those favoring and opposing safeguard measures, we spoke with attorneys representing both petitioners and respondents. We also interviewed Chinese government officials to obtain their perspective on the China safeguard. To examine the application of presidential discretion, we reviewed and analyzed the presidential determinations, and documents related to the legal challenge of one of these decisions. We compared the China safeguard with other safeguards throughout the report in order to provide context for understanding the outcomes so far. We performed our work from January 2004 to September 2005 in accordance with generally accepted government auditing standards. Appendix I contains a more detailed description of our scope and methodology.

---

[4]We have already published reports on both the China textile safeguard and the application of countervailing duties to China. GAO, *U.S.-China Trade: Textile Safeguard Procedures Should Be Improved,* GAO-05-296 (Washington D.C.: Apr. 4, 2005) and *U.S.-China Trade: Commerce Faces Practical and Legal Challenges in Applying Countervailing Duties,* GAO-05-474 (Washington D.C.: June 17, 2005). A forthcoming report will discuss antidumping measures against China.

Results in Brief

The China safeguard allows WTO members to restrict surging imports from China that cause market disruption to the domestic industry. In the United States, the safeguard is implemented by section 421 of the Trade Act of 1974,[5] which establishes a three-step process to consider its application. First, after receiving a petition, ITC determines whether there is market disruption by investigating whether imports from China have injured U.S. producers. If ITC does not find market disruption, the case ends. If ITC finds market disruption, it proposes a potential remedy for USTR's and the President's consideration. Second, USTR consults with China to seek an agreement that would address ITC's finding of market disruption. Concurrently, USTR obtains and evaluates information from interested parties on the appropriateness of any proposed remedy and makes a recommendation to the President. Finally, section 421 requires the President to provide relief unless he determines that doing so is not in the national economic interest, or would cause serious harm to U.S. national security. The China safeguard was modeled after the communist country safeguard and contains similar features. A number of these features differ from the U.S. global safeguard, which generally must be applied to products from all U.S. trading partners.

The United States has yet to apply the China safeguard, even though it has completed its consideration of five petitions for relief filed by U.S. producers. In a sixth case, ITC is expected to make a determination in early October 2005. In two instances, ITC found no market disruption and the cases ended. In the three other cases, ITC found market disruption and recommended a remedy to USTR and the President. In these three cases, USTR's consultations with the Chinese did not result in any agreements to address the market disruption. USTR held public hearings and heard testimony on a number of remedy options, including ITC-proposed tariffs, quotas, and not providing any relief. USTR evaluated the pros and cons of the various options and made a recommendation to the President. In all three cases, the President declined to provide relief because he found it would not be in the national economic interest of the United States. Presidents have made similar decisions to deny relief under the communist country safeguard. In contrast, Presidents have granted relief in half of the global safeguard cases in which ITC recommended relief, and in all such cases after Congress revised U.S. trade law in 1988.

---

[5]19 U.S.C. § 2451.

The President's decisions not to provide import relief after ITC found market disruption generated controversy, including a legal challenge to his first safeguard decision before the U.S. Court of International Trade claiming that he exceeded his authority. The legislative history of section 421 shows that the relevant committee intended that there would be a presumption in favor of the President's providing relief once ITC found market disruption. While section 421 court held that the President still has broad discretion not to apply the China safeguard. Furthermore, the President considers the question of whether to provide relief from a broader perspective than ITC, which focuses on the domestic industry. In contrast, the President focuses on the national economic interest when weighing the benefits of relief against the costs, and considers factors such as the effect on consumers and downstream users, which ITC does not. Furthermore, the President cited third-country imports in all his decisions denying relief under both the Chinese and communist country safeguards. Conversely, under the global safeguard, third-country imports generally cannot diminish the potential benefits of import relief to the domestic industry. The President's decisions have been different under the global safeguard.

We provided ITC and USTR a draft of this report for their review and comment. Both agencies chose to provide technical comments from their staff. We incorporated their suggestions as appropriate.

Background

In general, safeguards are temporary import restrictions that provide an opportunity for domestic industries to adjust to increasing imports. Both the WTO Agreement on Safeguards and article XIX of the General Agreement on Tariffs and Trade establish general rules for the application of safeguard measures. Safeguard actions taken under the WTO usually apply to all imports of a product irrespective of source.[6] Other multilateral and bilateral trade agreements also contain safeguard provisions. China's WTO accession agreement is an example of such an agreement. Its provisions contain a transitional product-specific safeguard that permits WTO members, including the United States, to take measures to address disruptive import surges from China alone. Under the terms of China's WTO accession agreement, members may use the China safeguard until 2013.

---

[6]WTO Agreement on Safeguards, art. 2.2.

In addition to the China safeguard, three other safeguards have been applied to imports from that country in the United States. First, a communist country safeguard applied to China prior to its WTO accession and still applies to import surges from other communist countries that are not WTO members.[7] Second, Chinese imports are subject to a U.S. global safeguard that applies to all WTO members.[8] Third, a textile safeguard provided for in China's WTO accession agreement covers textile and apparel imports from China.[9]

U.S. Law Establishes Three-Step Process for China Safeguard Decisions

In the United States, the China safeguard is implemented under section 421 of the Trade Act of 1974, as amended, which Congress enacted as part of the legislation authorizing the President to grant China permanent normal trade relations status.[10] Under section 421, U.S. firms may petition the government to apply a China safeguard. The section establishes a three-step process to consider China safeguard petitions. This three-step process involves ITC, USTR, and the President, and it results in determinations about whether import surges from China have caused market disruption and whether a remedy is in the national economic interest or, in extraordinary circumstances, would cause serious harm to national security. The entire process takes approximately 150 days (see fig. 1).[11] The China safeguard was modeled on the communist country safeguard, which applied to China before it became a WTO member.

---

[7] The communist country safeguard is set forth under section 406 of the Trade Act of 1974.

[8] In the United States, the global safeguard is set forth in section 201 of the Trade Act of 1974 and is sometimes referred to as the "escape clause" or the "section 201 safeguard."

[9] GAO-05-296.

[10] Pub. L. No. 106-286, 114 Stat. 880.

[11] Petitioners may claim "critical circumstances" and seek that provisional relief be provided within 65 days. 19 U.S.C. § 2451(i).

Figure 1: China Safeguard Timeline

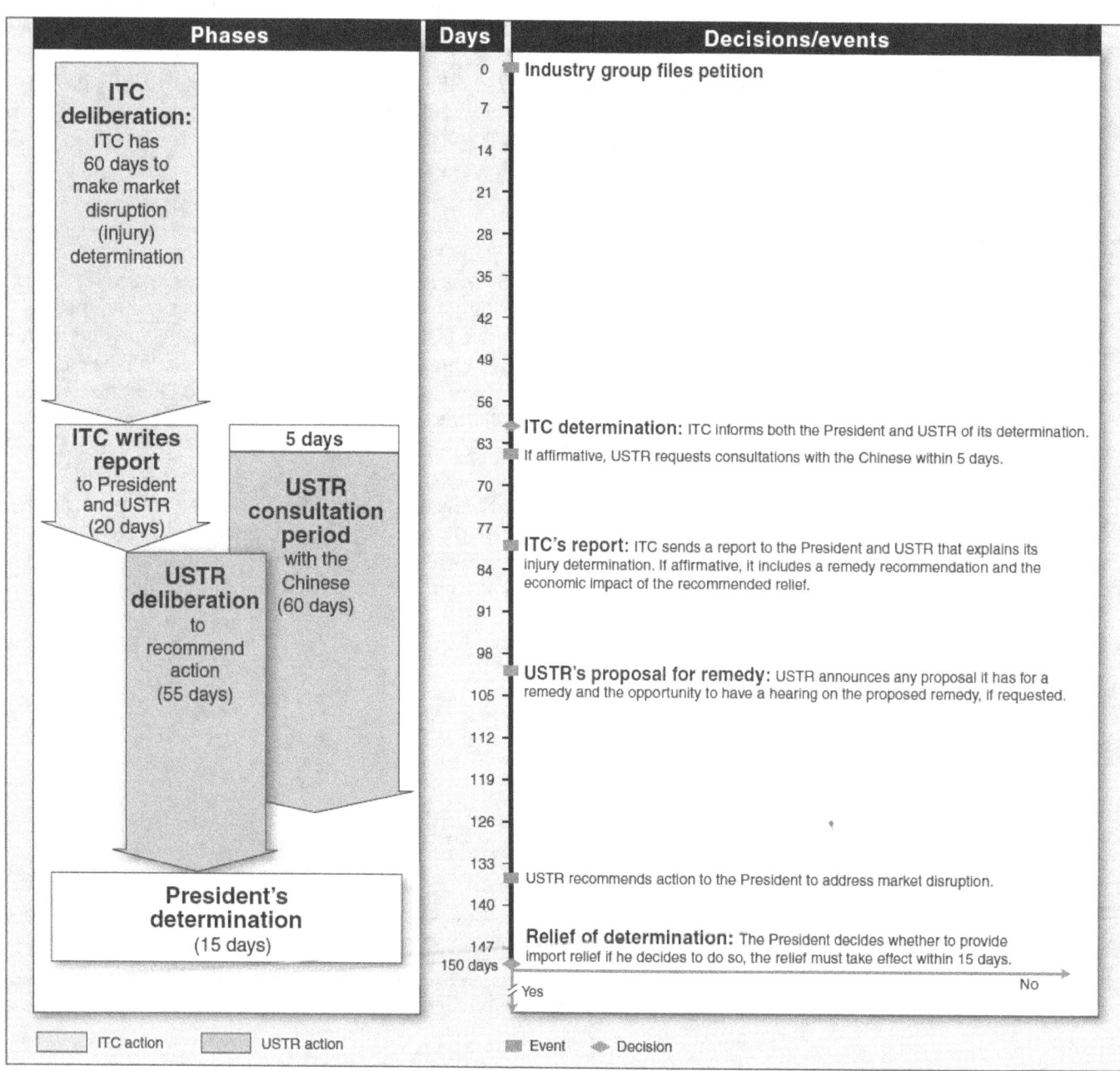

Sources: GAO analysis of information provided by USTR and ITC.

Note: The President, USTR, the House Committee on Ways and Means, and the Senate Committee on Finance may also request an investigation. Time frames vary if "critical circumstances" are involved.

U.S. Producers May File Petitions Claiming Market Disruption Due to Chinese Imports	U.S. producers and certain other entities may file petitions to initiate China safeguard investigations with ITC. These include trade associations, firms, certified or recognized unions, or groups of workers that represent an industry. The President, USTR, the Senate Committee on Finance, and the House of Representatives' Committee on Ways and Means can also request investigations.[12]

The petition must include certain information supporting a claim that imports from China are causing market disruption to an industry. Petitions must include, among other things, the following: product description, import data, domestic production data, and data showing injury. Petitions must also include information on all known producers in China and the type of import relief sought.

The Role of ITC Is to Determine Market Disruption and Recommend a Remedy	ITC determines whether imports from China are causing market disruption to U.S. producers and, if so, recommends a remedy to address it. Upon receiving a petition, ITC initiates an investigation by publishing a notice in the *Federal Register* and holding public hearings to afford interested parties the opportunity to present information. ITC receives information on both market disruption and potential remedies from parties through written submission and oral testimony. ITC has 60 days to determine whether the imports from China are causing–or threatening to cause–market disruption to domestic producers.

More specifically, ITC must determine whether imports from China are entering the United States in "such increased quantities or under such conditions as to cause or threaten to cause market disruption" to domestic producers. According to section 421, to determine that market disruption exists ITC must make the following three findings:

- Imports of the subject product from China are increasing rapidly, either absolutely or relatively.

- The domestic industry is materially injured or threatened with material injury.

- Such rapidly increasing imports are a significant cause of the material injury or threat of material injury.

---

[12]*Id.* §§ 2451(b) and 2252(a).

If a majority of ITC commissioners determine that market disruption does not exist, the case ends.[13] After an affirmative determination, ITC must propose a remedy. This could include the imposition of a duty, or an additional duty, or another import restriction (such as a quota) necessary to prevent or remedy the market disruption.

Within 20 days after making a determination of market disruption, ITC must transmit a report to the President and USTR. The ITC report must include the determination, the reasons for it, recommendations of proposed remedies, and any dissenting or separate views of commissioners. The report must also describe the short- and long-term effects that recommended remedies are likely to have on the petitioning domestic industry, other domestic industries, and consumers. In addition, the report must describe the short- and long-term effects of not taking the recommended action on the petitioning domestic industry, its workers, the communities where production facilities of the industry are located, and on other domestic industries.

The Role of USTR Is to Make a Recommendation to the President

If ITC renders an affirmative determination, USTR undertakes two parallel efforts. First, USTR consults with China about ITC's finding and seeks to reach an agreement that would prevent or remedy the market disruption.[14] If the U.S. and Chinese governments do not reach agreement after 60 days (or if the President determines that an agreement reached is not addressing the market disruption), the United States may then apply a safeguard.

Concurrently, USTR obtains and evaluates information from interested parties on the appropriateness of ITC's or any other proposed remedy and makes a recommendation to the President. Within 20 days after receiving the ITC report, USTR issues a *Federal Register* notice to solicit comments from the public (e.g., importers and consumers). USTR must hold a public hearing if requested to do so. USTR evaluates the information it receives and consults with the other agencies of the Trade Policy Staff Committee

---

[13]If the commissioners are equally divided with respect to injury, the President can consider either finding (negative or affirmative) as the ITC determination.

[14]There is some overlap between the ITC and USTR phases of the process. The ITC has 60 days to determine whether there is market disruption. After that it has 20 days to formulate a remedy to the market disruption found to exist. USTR must request consultations within 5 days after receiving the market disruption determination.

(TPSC).[15] Within 55 days after receiving the ITC report, USTR must make a recommendation to the President about what action, if any, to take to prevent or remedy market disruption.

The Role of the President Is to Decide Whether Relief Is in the National Interest

Under section 421 the President makes the final decision on the provision of import relief. Within 15 days after receiving a USTR recommendation, the President must decide whether and to what extent to provide relief. Section 421 states: "the President shall provide import relief... unless the President determines that provision of such relief is not in the national economic interest of the United States or, in extraordinary cases, that the taking of action... would cause serious harm to the national security of the United States." Although the law does not define "national economic interest," it further states that the President may determine "that providing import relief is not in the national economic interest of the United States only if [he] finds that the taking of such action would have an adverse impact on the United States economy clearly greater than the benefits of such action." Finally, section 421 requires the President to publish his decision and the reasons for it in the *Federal Register*.[16]

China Safeguard Modeled on Communist Country Safeguard

The China safeguard was modeled on the communist country safeguard. In fact, according to its legislative history, it was intended to replace the communist country safeguard for China since it would no longer apply once China became a member of the WTO. As shown in table 1 below, the safeguards share several important characteristics. Both safeguards are limited in scope to imports from particular countries; while the former is limited to imports from China, the latter is limited to imports from one or more communist countries. They also share similar criteria with regard to ITC market disruption determinations and identify the President as final decision maker on whether to provide relief. In addition, both safeguards have a 150-day determination period.

In contrast, the China safeguard is significantly different from the global safeguard. The China safeguard is narrower in scope than the global

---

[15]The TPSC is the mechanism by which USTR consults with other agencies on trade policy matters.

[16]19 U.S.C. § 2451(l). Section 421 also authorizes the President to modify, reduce, or terminate the safeguard relief that he imposed. On the other hand, the President can also extend the effective period of the safeguard action. *Id.* § 2451(n) and (o).

safeguard; it can only be applied to imports from that one country, whereas the global safeguard generally must be applied to all foreign sources of a particular product. Also, the China safeguard's market disruption standard is regarded to be easier to meet than the criteria for determining injury due to imports under the global safeguard. [17] Furthermore, the standard for presidential action is also different under the global safeguard as it places more emphasis on assisting the domestic industries' efforts to adjust to international competition (including worker adjustments), and sets forth a broader range of factors for the President to consider in determining whether to provide relief. Finally, the time frame for the China safeguard process is shorter than the global safeguard.

---

[17] See S. Rep. No. 93-1299, at 212 (1974) and 146 Cong. Rec. 18,112 (2000) (statement of Sen. Collins which included a September 7, 2000 letter from then-U.S. Trade Representative Charlene Barshefsky to Sen. Collins).

Table 1: Comparison of China, Communist Country, and Global Safeguards

	China safeguard (section 421) effective in December 2001	Communist country safeguard (section 406) enacted in 1974	Global safeguard (section 201) enacted in 1974[a]
Scope	Imports from China	Imports from a communist country	Imports from all foreign sources
Injury standard	significant cause of material injury or threat thereof	significant cause of material injury or threat thereof	substantial cause of serious injury or threat thereof
Presidential standard	"...the President shall provide import relief for such industry ...unless the President determines that provision of such relief is not in the national economic interest of the United States or, in extraordinary cases, would cause serious harm to the national security of the United States."	"...the President must provide import relief, unless he determines that relief is not in the national economic interest."	"...the President shall take all appropriate and feasible action within his power which the President determines will facilitate efforts by the domestic industry to make a positive adjustment to import competition and provide greater economic and social benefits than costs."
ITC statutory time frame	80 days	3 months	180 days
USTR statutory time frame	55 days	N/A	N/A[b]
Presidential statutory time frame	15 days	75 days[c]	60 days

Source: GAO.

[a]Congress amended the standard for presidential action for the global safeguard in the Omnibus Trade and Competitiveness Act of 1988, Pub. L. No. 100-418, 102 Stat. 1225.

[b]The Trade Policy Staff Committee must advise the President; however, no specific time frame is outlined in the statute.

[c]The President has an additional 60 days to negotiate an orderly marketing agreement, if necessary.

Note: Time frames vary if "critical circumstances" are involved.

N/A=Not applicable.

The United States Has Never Applied the China Safeguard

Between August 2002 and September 2005, the United States considered five petitions from domestic producers to apply the China safeguard but it has not provided relief. ITC made negative determinations on two petitions and, in three other cases, found market disruption and recommended restricting imports to remedy the situation, ITC is expected to make a determination in a sixth case in early October 2005. In each of the three cases where ITC found market disruption, USTR formulated a presidential recommendation after evaluating various options. The President then decided not to provide any import relief. The success rate for China safeguard petitions is similar to communist country safeguard petitions, but differs from that of global safeguard petitions.

U.S. Firms Filed Six Petitions

U.S. firms have filed six petitions for China safeguard relief since section 421 was enacted (see fig. 2). The petitioners representing the domestic industry ranged from one firm in two cases to seven firms and a union in the most recent petition. The products involved are the following:

- pedestal actuators (for raising and lowering seats in mobility scooters),

- certain steel wire garment hangers,

- brake drums and rotors,

- ductile iron waterworks fittings (for municipal water systems),

- uncovered innersprings used in mattresses, and

- circular welded nonalloy steel pipes.

Figure 2: Dates of China Safeguard Petitions

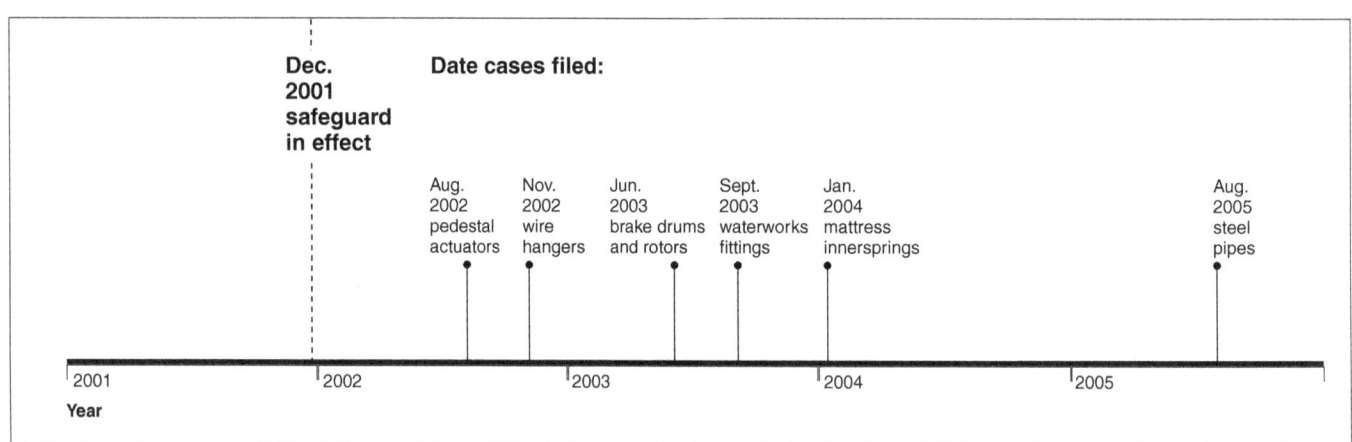

Source: GAO analysis of ITC *Federal Register* notices.

ITC Found Market Disruption in Three of Five Cases

ITC made negative determinations in two of five completed China safeguard cases.[18] In cases brought by manufacturers of brake drums and rotors and mattress innersprings, ITC determined that Chinese imports

---

[18]ITC is expected to make a determination in the steel pipes case in early October 2005.

had not disrupted the domestic market. More specifically, in the brake drums and rotors case, ITC found that although imports from China were increasing rapidly, the domestic industry was neither materially injured nor threatened with material injury. In the mattress innerspring case, ITC was divided on the reasons for making a negative determination. Three of the commissioners determined that imports from China were not increasing rapidly. The other three commissioners determined that the domestic industry was not materially injured or threatened with material injury. In both cases, ITC cited the industries' healthy profit margins and stable or rising prices as evidence that neither industry was materially injured or threatened with material injury.

In the remaining three cases (pedestal actuators, wire hangers, and waterworks fittings), ITC found market disruption and recommended measures to remedy it. In all three cases, ITC cited factors such as falling production and employment in its determinations that the industry was materially injured. Furthermore, ITC noted declines in the industries' health that coincided with a surge in Chinese imports when they determined that rapidly increasing imports from China were a significant cause of material injury. In other words, Chinese imports caused market disruption to the domestic industry. In deciding which import restriction to recommend, ITC considered the conditions of competition in the domestic industry (e.g., demand conditions, and import and domestic supply conditions), as well as comments received from parties in the cases.

ITC recommended different import restrictions to remedy the market disruption it found in each case. For example, as noted in table 2 below, ITC found that a 3-year, declining tariff on wire hangers from China was the most appropriate remedy in that case. In contrast, ITC recommended a 3-year quota in the pedestal actuator case because there was only one supplier and one primary purchaser of pedestal actuators, and the domestic-imported price differential was large. In addition, the ITC also proposed that the President direct the Departments of Commerce and Labor to provide expedited consideration of trade adjustment assistance applications for workers in the wire hangers and waterworks fittings industries.

Table 2: Results of ITC China Safeguard Investigations (2002-2005)

Product name	Number of firms	Value of imports	ITC market disruption vote	ITC majority remedy recommendation
Brake drums and rotors	3-firm coalition	Brake drums: $13,090,000 Brake rotors: $166,228,000 (2002)	4-0 negative	N/A
Mattress innersprings	4	$5,894,000 (2003)	6-0 negative	N/A
Wire hangers	3	$8,814,000 (2001)	5-0 affirmative	3-year duty in addition to the current duty (25% in year 1; 20% in year 2; and 15% in year 3).
Waterworks fittings	1	$22,656,000 (2002)	6-0 affirmative	3-year tariff-rate quota, in addition to the current rate of duty (50% duty on imports above 14,324 short tons in year 1; 40% tariff on imports above 15,398 short tons in year 2; and 30% tariff on imports above 16,553 short tons in year 3).
Pedestal actuators	1	Number not publicly available	3-2 affirmative	3-year quantitative restriction (5,626 units in year 1; 6,470 units in year 2; and 7,440 units in year 3).

Sources: ITC staff reports and views of the commissioners.

Note: Value of imports in last full year before investigation.

USTR Consulted with Chinese, Sought Comments, and Considered Multiple Options

USTR consulted with the Chinese government, solicited and obtained comments from a variety of sources, and analyzed the advantages and disadvantages of the ITC remedies and other options in formulating its recommendations to the President.

After receiving each of the three affirmative market disruption determinations from ITC, USTR requested consultations with the Chinese government. USTR notified the WTO Committee on Safeguards of the consultation requests. Representatives of the two governments met but did not reach any agreements to address the market disruption found by ITC, according to USTR officials. During the 60-day consultation period, USTR continued to gather information from interested parties about any potential remedies.

USTR, in conjunction with other agencies on the TPSC, held a 1-day public hearing for each of the cases and obtained views on what, if any, type of import restriction was in the public interest. The parties also had the opportunity to provide written comments. In addition to the ITC-recommended remedies, USTR sought comment on alternate remedies and on not providing relief. The hearings included both the domestic petitioners and Chinese respondents, as well as other interested parties such as importers and downstream users. For example, the wire hanger hearing included testimony from a hanger distributor. In the pedestal actuator and wire hanger cases, a representative from the Chinese government testified that applying the safeguard would damage U.S.-China bilateral economic relations, in addition to raising procedural and substantive concerns.[19] USTR officials said that certain information relevant to the effectiveness of potential remedies surfaced at these hearings, that did not surface in the ITC proceedings.

After the hearings, the USTR staff weighed the pros and cons of the various courses of action. USTR considered ITC's analysis, as well as the testimony and written submissions provided by interested parties, and sought comments from other TPSC members. According to detailed briefings from USTR officials, in each case USTR considered the ITC-recommended remedy among other remedies presented, as well as the option of having no remedy. USTR staff worked with the U.S. Trade Representative throughout the proceedings. USTR staff then drafted a recommendation in a memorandum to the U.S. Trade Representative, who assessed the various options. The Trade Representative then made a recommendation in a memorandum to the President.

President Decided Not to Apply the China Safeguard

The President declined to provide relief in all three cases.[20] He found that imposing remedies such as duties and quotas would not be in the national economic interest. The President's reasons for not providing relief were printed in the *Federal Register* and are summarized in table 3. The President's decisions did not cite national security concerns as a reason in any of the three cases.

---

[19]For example, in both cases the Chinese government argued that any remedy imposed would be ineffective because it would not help the petitioners and would harm U.S. consumers.

[20]In the wire hangers case, the President directed the Secretary of Commerce and the Secretary of Labor to expedite consideration of any Trade Adjustment Assistance applications received from domestic hanger producers or their workers and to provide such other requested assistance or relief as they deemed appropriate, consistent with their statutory mandate.

Table 3: Reasons Cited by the President in Decisions Not to Provide Import Relief

Case	Reasons by the President
Pedestal actuators	Imposing the ITC's recommended quota would not benefit the domestic producing industry and would cause imports to shift from China to other offshore sources.
	The cost of the quota to downstream users and consumers would substantially outweigh the benefit to producer's income.
	Relief would negatively impact workers in downstream industries, which have a significantly larger number of workers than the domestic pedestal actuator industry.
	Relief would negatively affect disabled and elderly purchasers of mobility scooters and electric wheelchairs.
Wire hangers	Imposing additional tariffs on Chinese imports would affect domestic producers unevenly.
	Domestic producers have already begun to pursue adjustment strategies.
	Domestic producers have a dominant share of the market and thus have the opportunity to adjust to competition from Chinese imports even without import relief.
	There is a strong possibility that if additional tariffs were imposed, production would shift to third countries.
	Additional tariffs would have an uneven impact on domestic distributors of wire hangers.
	Additional tariffs would likely have a negative effect on small dry-cleaning businesses.
Waterworks fittings	A remedy would be ineffective because imports from third countries would likely replace curtailed Chinese imports.
	Import relief would cost U.S. consumers substantially more than the increased income realized by domestic producers.
	Domestic producers enjoy a strong competitive position in the U.S. market.[a]
	In 2002 and 2003, imports of this product have been relatively stable in volume terms and declined slightly in value terms.[a]

Source: GAO summaries of presidential determinations of January 17, 2003, April 25, 2003, and March 3, 2004.

[a]The President noted that this reason was not necessary in reaching his determination.

China and Communist Country Safeguard Outcomes Differ from Global Safeguard

The final outcomes of China safeguard cases are similar to those of communist country[21] safeguard cases but different than global safeguard cases. As shown in table 4, domestic industries have sought relief under the China and communist country safeguards far less frequently than they have sought relief under the global safeguard. Overall, petitioners have been denied relief in almost all China and communist country safeguard cases but have been granted import relief in about one quarter of global safeguard cases. Of those cases where ITC found the industry was injured by imports, the President denied relief in all but one of the China and communist country safeguard cases. Conversely, the President granted

---

[21]There is no statutory list of communist countries. Petitioners have brought cases against the following countries: Romania, China, USSR, Poland, and East Germany.

relief in about half of the global safeguard cases where the ITC found injury. Moreover, since Congress amended the global safeguard's standard for presidential action in the 1988 Trade Act, the President has always provided relief when ITC found injury.

Table 4: Outcomes of Completed China, Communist Country, and Global Safeguard Cases (as of September 2005)

	China safeguard	Communist country safeguard[a]	Global safeguard[b]
Number of cases since enacted	5	13[c]	73
ITC determination			
• **Affirmative**	3	4	34
• **Tie vote**[d]	0	1	6
• **Negative**	2	7	32
• **Terminated**	0	1	1
Presidential decision on import relief			
• **Provided**	0	1[e]	19[f]
• **Not provided**	3	4[g]	21

Source: GAO analysis of ITC import injury investigation statistics and presidential determinations.

[a]Since section 406 was modified by the Omnibus Trade and Competitiveness Act of 1988, there have been only two petitions. One case was terminated; in the other, the ITC made an affirmative injury determination and the President denied relief.

[b]Since section 201 was modified by the Trade Act of 1988, there have been 13 petitions.

[c]China has been the target of 7 out of the 13 section 406 cases brought by petitioners.

[d]In the case of a tie vote, the President may accept either an affirmative or negative determination.

[e]The President directed the U.S. Trade Representative to negotiate an orderly marketing agreement with China.

[f]With respect to the six tie votes referred to him under the global safeguard, the President provided import relief in one case.

[g]In the one section 406 case in which the ITC commissioners were evenly divided, the President took no action to restrict imports.

The President Has Exercised His Broad Discretion in Deciding Not to Apply Relief

The President's decisions not to impose relief in the three China safeguard cases in which ITC found market disruption have been criticized. Nevertheless, the President has broad discretionary authority under section 421 to consider U.S. national economic and security interests when weighing the facts and circumstances particular to each case. This broad discretion was upheld by the U.S. Court of International Trade. This, together with the fact that the President considers factors that ITC does not, including consumer cost and the potential for imports from other countries, allows him to reject relief even when it has been recommended by ITC.

Presidential Decisions Not to Apply Safeguards Have Generated Controversy

Several different groups have criticized the President's decisions not to apply China safeguard relief. For example, company officials and trade lawyers who were unsuccessful in obtaining relief criticized the President's decisions in several congressional hearings. As we discuss later, one company subsequently filed a lawsuit against the President claiming he exceeded his authority in rejecting ITC's recommended remedy.

In July 2005, legislation was introduced in Congress to change the President's discretion.[22] Some congressmen expressed disapproval over the President's decisions based on the fact that ITC made unanimous, affirmative determinations in two of these cases. One representative in particular argued that the President was not following the intent of the law in rejecting the safeguard actions. Also, 21 other House members wrote the President stating their belief that Congress had carefully limited the President's discretion to deny relief. In this regard, the legislative history of section 421 shows that the House Committee on Ways and Means intended a presumption in favor of relief. The House report stated:

The bill establishes clear standards for the application of Presidential discretion in providing relief to injured industries and workers. If the ITC makes an affirmative determination on market disruption, there would be a presumption in favor of providing relief. That presumption can be overcome only if the President finds that providing relief would have an adverse impact on the United States economy clearly greater than the benefits of such action, or, in extraordinary cases, that such action would cause serious harm to the national security of the United States.[23]

This legislative history, together with the China safeguard's shorter time frames and lesser injury standard, and other procedural characteristics, may have created an expectation that the likelihood for relief under the China safeguard was going to be greater compared with the global safeguard.

---

[22]H.R. 3306, 109 Cong., 1st Sess. (2005).

[23]H.R. Rep. No. 106-632, at 18 (2000).

Similarly, the U.S.-China Economic and Security Review Commission, a body established by Congress to monitor and investigate the security and economic implications of the bilateral economic relationship between the United States and China, held hearings and criticized the administration for failing to apply the safeguard after an affirmative ITC injury determination. In March 2005, this commission recommended that Congress consider amending the China safeguard to either eliminate the President's discretion or limit it to the consideration of noneconomic national security factors after an affirmative ITC finding.

In addition, the lack of any positive decisions by the President in these cases may have discouraged other U.S. producers from seeking relief under the China safeguard. Several trade lawyers representing domestic U.S. producers with whom we spoke told us about their reluctance to bring additional China safeguard cases in the future because they thought that the President would reject them based on political considerations. The U.S.-China Economic Security Review Commission expressed similar concern that repeated presidential refusal to apply the safeguard had undermined the instrument's efficacy. Indeed, until August 2005, when producers filed a petition on steel pipe, no China safeguard petition had been filed since March 2004, when the President rejected an ITC recommendation to provide relief from imports of Chinese ductile iron waterworks fittings.

Court Has Found that the President Has Broad Statutory Discretion

Despite criticisms, the President's discretion under the China safeguard is quite broad. The President must provide relief unless he finds that it is not in the national economic or security interest. With regard to the former, the President is authorized to deny relief when he finds that the relief would have an adverse impact on the United States economy clearly greater than the benefits.

In June 2004, the U.S. Court of International Trade affirmed the President's broad discretionary authority in a case brought by the petitioner in the first China product safeguard case.[24] In that case, Motion Systems Corp. contended that the President had exceeded his authority under section 421 by not providing relief. In particular, Motion Systems argued that the President was required to quantify the adverse impact of providing relief and demonstrate that the adverse impact was clearly greater than the

---

[24]*Motion Systems Corp. v. Bush*, 342 F. Supp. 2d 1247 (C.I.T. 2004).

benefits that the relief would provide to the domestic industry. In this regard, Motion Systems maintained that section 421 created a presumption of relief once ITC made an affirmative determination of market disruption.[25]

In affirming the President's decision,[26] the Court held that the President had not exceeded his authority and said the law granted him "considerable discretion."[27] The Court found that section 421 made no reference to evidence or a burden of proof that the President must satisfy to support his conclusion that the imposition of a safeguard would have an adverse impact on the U.S. economy clearly greater than its benefits.[28] The Court also noted that the President was not prohibited from considering political factors in making a finding about the adverse impact on the U.S. economy, including trade relations between the United States and China.[29] Finally, the Court did not specifically comment on the presumption of relief issue.

President Considers a Broader Range of Factors than ITC

While ITC makes remedy recommendations that would alleviate market disruption, the President considers a broader range of factors than ITC in determining whether to apply China safeguard relief. Specifically, under section 421, ITC focuses on the *domestic industry* involved in the proceeding, both in the context of making injury determinations and recommendations for relief. For example, among the factors ITC considered in determining material injury were the idling of U.S. production facilities and the ability of firms within the industry to produce at reasonable profit, wage, and employment levels.[30] Thus, ITC did not

---

[25]In making this argument Motion Systems relied, in part, on the language in the House Report, quoted above in the text.

[26]An appeal of the decision is pending before the Court of Appeals for the Federal Circuit.

[27]The Court's analysis focused on the standard of review the Court should apply in reviewing presidential actions under U.S. trade statutes. 342 F.Supp. at 1258-67.

[28]In this regard, the Court disagreed that the "clearly greater" language requires that the evidence supporting the President's denial must be "clear and convincing," "beyond a reasonable doubt," or "more-than-substantial." *Id.* 1261-62.

[29]Nevertheless, the Court found that neither the record before it, nor the text of the President's decision, established that trade relations between the United States and China were a factor in the President's decision. *Id.* at 1265-66.

[30]The ITC commissioners have noted in their determinations that they do not consider any one factor dispositive. E.g., *Pedestal Actuators from China*, Inv. No. TA-421-1, USITC Pub. 3557 at 13 (Nov. 2002).

weigh the interests of other groups such as consumers and downstream industries against potential benefits to the domestic industry when developing its recommendations for the President to consider. [31] Nevertheless, ITC reports on the potential economic effect of its recommended remedies, as described earlier. However, section 421, does not require ITC to consider these broad economic effects when developing its recommendations.

In contrast, as discussed above, section 421 authorizes the President to consider *overall U.S. economic and security interests* in deciding whether to impose China safeguard relief. [32] In each of the three cases where ITC found injury and recommended a remedy, the President found, among other things, that relief would have an adverse impact on other participants in the economy. The President determined that relief would carry substantial costs for consumers or downstream users of the products involved. Specifically, the President cited the increased costs to aged and disabled consumers of mobility scooters as a reason for not providing relief in the pedestal actuator case. In the wire hangers case, the President stated that relief would have an uneven impact on wire hanger distributors and impose increased costs on dry cleaning companies. Finally, in the waterworks fittings case, the President found that the costs to consumers would substantially outweigh producer income benefits.

The President's decisions also took into account the unique facts and circumstances in each case. For example, in the pedestal actuator case there was only one petitioner seeking relief and one dominant purchaser. In the wire hanger case, domestic producers had different business models that affected whether a remedy would benefit or disadvantage them. In addition, the U.S. Trade Representative noted in a March 2004 congressional hearing that, while not necessary to the President's decision, in the waterworks fittings case the petitioner faced serious problems besides competing Chinese imports. [33] Although the President did

---

[31]Furthermore, ITC's recommended remedies only address imports from China that caused market disruption.

[32]In making its required recommendations to the President about what, if any, action to take to prevent or remedy market disruption, USTR informed us that it both considers a broader range of information about the domestic industry involved than ITC, as well as broader national economic factors.

[33]President Bush's Trade Agenda: Hearing Before the House Comm. on Ways and Means, 108th Cong. 43 (2004)(statement of Robert Zoellick, United States Trade Representative).

GAO-05-1056 U.S.-China Trade

not provide import relief in these cases, he stated that he remains committed to applying the China safeguard when circumstances warrant.

President Cites Third Country Imports When Denying Relief

The President has considered whether relief would benefit the producers involved in every case.[34] In his decisions denying relief the President stated that imposing a safeguard would have limited benefits. One factor that the President has cited in all three cases is that applying a safeguard would lead to production being shifted from China to other countries rather than to U.S. producers. In the waterworks fittings case, the President specifically identified other current suppliers to the U.S. market such as India, Brazil, Korea, and Mexico.

Similarly, in all but one communist country safeguard determinations, the President found, among other things, that providing relief would have resulted in imports shifting from the communist country involved to other offshore sources. With only one exception, the President has never approved a remedy under the communist country safeguard. In contrast, under the global safeguard, imports from other countries generally cannot diminish the potential benefits of import relief.[35] Since the global safeguard statute was enacted in 1974, the President applied relief in approximately half of the cases in which ITC has made a positive injury determination. Moreover, since it was substantially amended in 1988, the President has provided relief in every such global safeguard case. It is not possible to identify all the factors that contribute to such opposite results among the different safeguards. However, one consistent factor has been that the China and communist country safeguards, respectively, are limited in scope to products from one or a few countries; this allows other foreign sources to gain market share of the product and reduce the potential benefit of the safeguard to the domestic producers.

[34]A USTR official testified in April 2005 that the extent to which relief would benefit the domestic producers was "first and foremost" among the economic factors that the administration examines in deciding whether to impose relief.

[35]In global safeguards, the United States excludes developing country imports that fall below a threshold level, and under varying circumstances may also exclude imports from countries with which it has entered into a free trade agreement, such as Canada and Mexico.

GAO-05-1056 U.S.-China Trade

Agency Comments and Our Evaluation

We provided ITC and USTR a draft of this report for their review and comment. Both agencies chose to provide technical comments from their staff. USTR staff cautioned against drawing overall conclusions about the use of the China safeguard given the small number of cases considered thus far. Additionally, both USTR and ITC staff suggested we clarify our characterizations of section 421's legislative history and of the *Motion Systems Corp. v. Bush* lawsuit. We modified the report in response to their suggestions. USTR and ITC also provided other suggestions to make the report more accurate and clear, which we incorporated as appropriate.

We are sending copies of this report to ITC and USTR, appropriate congressional committees, and other interested parties. We will also make copies available to others upon request. In addition, the report will be available at no charge on the GAO Web site at http://www.gao.gov.

If you or any of your staff have any questions about this report, please contact me at (202) 512-4347 or yagerl@gao.gov. Contact points for our Offices of Congressional Relations and Public Affairs may be found on the last page of this report. GAO staff who made major contributions to this report are listed in appendix II.

Loren Yager
Director, International Affairs and Trade

Appendix I: Objectives, Scope, and Methodology

To address our objectives, we reviewed U.S. laws and procedures as well as relevant World Trade Organization (WTO) agreements and China's accession agreement. To ensure our understanding of relevant laws, procedures, and agreements, we spoke with officials from the Office of the United States Trade Representative (USTR) and the International Trade Commission (ITC). In addition, we interviewed officials from the WTO and officials from the government of China. Finally, we spoke with law firms that had direct experience in China safeguard cases, as well as law firms with broad experience in trade actions against China.

To describe how the safeguard has been applied thus far, we examined each phase of the process. For the ITC phase, we reviewed and analyzed each of the determinations the ITC commissioners issued during the five China safeguard injury investigations completed as of July 31, 2005, to understand the rationale behind them. We further obtained private sector views of the ITC process by speaking with law firms that had represented petitioners and/or respondents in each of the five China safeguard injury investigations. For the USTR phase of the process, we spoke with law firms that had represented petitioners and/or respondents that participated in each of the three China safeguard remedy investigations and reviewed the transcripts of all three USTR hearings. USTR neither made the documents related to their analyses nor their recommendations available to us. Instead, we relied on detailed briefings from USTR officials on the nature and substance of their deliberations culminating in a recommendation to the President. For the presidential phase of the process, we reviewed each of the President's three determinations made under the China safeguard. To compare the use of the China safeguard with the communist country and global safeguards, we reviewed ITC import injury investigation statistics and presidential determinations in the China, communist country, and global safeguard cases. We found the ITC injury statistics to be sufficiently reliable for presenting and contrasting ITC's final disposition of cases brought under these statutes.

To examine the issues related to the application of presidential discretion, we analyzed the reasons the President gave in his decisions not to provide import relief. Additionally, we reviewed the legislative history of the China safeguard and written and oral testimony before Congress and the U.S.-China Economic and Security Review Commission. We reviewed the Court of International Trade's decision in the Motion Systems case against the government and the submissions of parties to the case. Finally, we

analyzed the presidential determinations made under the communist
country and global safeguards.[1]

---

[1]We confined our analysis of presidential determinations under section 201 of the Trade
Act of 1974 to those made after 1988 when Congress substantially amended the law.

Appendix II: GAO Contact and Staff Acknowledgments

GAO Contact	Loren Yager (202) 512-4347
Staff Acknowledgments	In addition to the individual named above, Adam R. Cowles, R. Gifford Howland, Michael McAtee, and Richard Seldin made significant contributions to this report.

GAO's Mission	The Government Accountability Office, the audit, evaluation and investigative arm of Congress, exists to support Congress in meeting its constitutional responsibilities and to help improve the performance and accountability of the federal government for the American people. GAO examines the use of public funds; evaluates federal programs and policies; and provides analyses, recommendations, and other assistance to help Congress make informed oversight, policy, and funding decisions. GAO's commitment to good government is reflected in its core values of accountability, integrity, and reliability.
Obtaining Copies of GAO Reports and Testimony	The fastest and easiest way to obtain copies of GAO documents at no cost is through GAO's Web site (www.gao.gov). Each weekday, GAO posts newly released reports, testimony, and correspondence on its Web site. To have GAO e-mail you a list of newly posted products every afternoon, go to www.gao.gov and select "Subscribe to Updates."
Order by Mail or Phone	The first copy of each printed report is free. Additional copies are $2 each. A check or money order should be made out to the Superintendent of Documents. GAO also accepts VISA and Mastercard. Orders for 100 or more copies mailed to a single address are discounted 25 percent. Orders should be sent to: U.S. Government Accountability Office 441 G Street NW, Room LM Washington, D.C. 20548 To order by Phone: Voice: (202) 512-6000 TDD: (202) 512-2537 Fax: (202) 512-6061
To Report Fraud, Waste, and Abuse in Federal Programs	Contact: Web site: www.gao.gov/fraudnet/fraudnet.htm E-mail: fraudnet@gao.gov Automated answering system: (800) 424-5454 or (202) 512-7470
Congressional Relations	Gloria Jarmon, Managing Director, JarmonG@gao.gov (202) 512-4400 U.S. Government Accountability Office, 441 G Street NW, Room 7125 Washington, D.C. 20548
Public Affairs	Paul Anderson, Managing Director, AndersonP1@gao.gov (202) 512-4800 U.S. Government Accountability Office, 441 G Street NW, Room 7149 Washington, D.C. 20548

www.ingramcontent.com/pod-product-compliance
Lightning Source LLC
Chambersburg PA
CBHW080940290526
45795CB00007BA/2837